In Favor of Hatred

I0086640

K. M. Patten

In Favor of Hatred

Other books by K. M. Patten:

Indictments from the Convicted: Rants, Articles, Interviews and Essays
Staying ON During the Great Reset

Print ISBN 978-1-949267-87-7
ebook ISBN 978-1-949267-89-1

Cover design by Guy Corp, www.GrafixCorp.com

STAIRWAY≡PRESS

STAIRWAY PRESS—APACHE JUNCTION

www.stairwaypress.com
1000 West Apache Trail, Suite 126
Apache Junction, AZ 85120 USA

In Favor of Hatred

TWO OBSERVATIONS CAN be made almost instantly when one considers the concept of Hatred.

1) It has existed.
2) It resulted in a lot of violence and suffering throughout the history of mankind.

Acknowledging this, it might be easy to conclude that Hatred is *bad*, and therefore we should all reject it in favor of what is thought to be Hatred's opposite: *love*.

That popular notion falls apart quickly.

For one thing, not very many will go up to the parents of a child who was intentionally and violently abused and tell them they should love the perpetrator. Those parents hate the abuser, and most others understand this hate.

Another thing: if Hatred has existed in the human psyche for all these millennia, then our hardwiring is thick and tightly knotted, thus making an *off switch* difficult to find.

Finally, the paradox: who can love unexceptionally when the next person's hatred is moral and just?

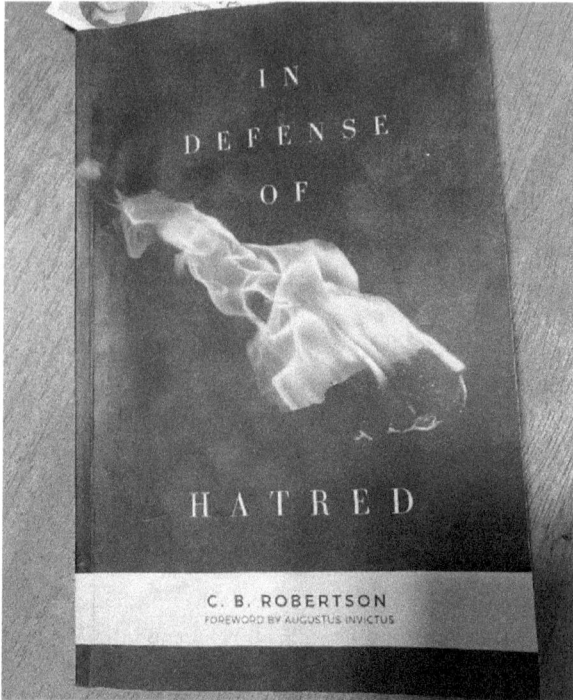

Still, the easily understandable example of the parent-child relationship—how hatred can stem from the desire to keep your loved ones safe—is one that C.B. Robertson also makes use of in his slender book *In Defense of Hatred*.[i]

He writes:

> *Hate is not opposed to love. It is inextricably derived from love, and is an expression of love.*

Robertson has a few decent points, but also leaves gaps which I hope to fill. Particularly, I will focus on the concepts of religion, war, racism, and *systems of power*.

Must hatred predate love?

If a drunk driver is on the road, and your family is walking on the sidewalk, does it require hatred to move your loved ones to safer distances, despite the drunk driver having no intention of harming anyone? Probably not (you might even be friends with someone who drives drunk routinely).

But if there's a convicted sexual predator lurking in your neighborhood and we anticipate their intentions, one might understand why that person would be hated, or at least hate their previous behavior. In this case, your child is no longer a random target, but one sought out with calculation.

Such ethical scenarios, common as they are, are not ones Robertson gives much thought to. Instead, he gives a more generalized argument, telling us why hatred has been a necessary emotion in preparation for combat.

Shakespeare and Roman history provide the groundwork, giving an unavoidable impression of what Robertson has in mind: war.

Against who? Defending what? Let's circle the wagons.

Chapter Two

ROBERTSON IS AT first dismissive of hatred if applied to anything other than people. Then he seems to contradict himself.

Robertson writes:

> *When a person is difficult to work with, or bothers us in some way but is not wronging us, they might be 'irritating,' or 'obnoxious,' but true anger is reserved for when we are wronged, and only conscious minds can do that.*

He then defines hatred as "disgust towards mind," going on to rebuff all claims of hatred for ideas and objects and places as mere "hyperbole," which are "in many cases, just a thin cover for cowardice":

> *Saying that you hate an idea is merely an evasion from saying you hate the people who create or implement the idea. Indeed you wouldn't even be aware of the idea unless someone was expressing it to you, by word or action. Because ideas are never the ones acting against you, hating an idea is as useful as being angry at the washing machine. I promise you the machine will not recognize the injustice, and the idea will not fear you.*
>
> *As for objects and places, "caution" and "dislike" are not synonymous with "hatred," in our experience of the feelings or how we act upon them. This is because there is no mind behind objects and places. Perhaps someone might genuinely feel "hate" towards some inanimate object, but we are no more obligated to take them seriously than we would if they were angry.*

I think this is incorrect. And as I'll show in a second, Robertson doesn't really believe it either.

Ideas are a perfectly acceptable target for hatred. Atheists are not irritated at the possible paper cuts given by a mishandling of the Bible; they hate the teachings contained in the Bible. Employing a classic parable, suppose there's an island out in the middle of the ocean. Living on this island is a single tribe that has existed for untold eons without the influence of any kind of external philosophy—not Marx nor Rothbard nor Christ. One day, a helicopter flies overhead, and down drops a selection of one of these belief systems, perfectly translated into the tribe's native tongue.

Then the helicopter leaves. If the texts are read and understood, preached and practiced, then one would be able to make certain predictions on how that society will look in a couple of generations' time. But perhaps the tribe is happy living a ludic lifestyle and doesn't want the industrial expanses generated by sophisticated economic theories. Or maybe they like worshipping their mountain god, and many of the tribesmen feel indifferent about Christ.

We can blame some people in the here and now: the members who tried propagating the ideas, the helicopter pilot who brought the ideas and everyone else who stood by and let the ideas take root.

And although it would still be justified to hate those who acted as mediums between the ideas and their implementation, it would be unreasonable to hate those who had drafted the ideas, as those philosophers are long dead. But if hatred can only be directed towards *conscious mind*, it's not too much of a stretch to hate the *crystallized form* of that conscious mind.

Why should this only be reserved for sentient beings

living at present, with their fluctuating motivations and easily-altered modes of thought? When people say that it's "easier to destroy than to build," they are correct only insofar as they are discussing physical monuments; but destroying ideas is a much harder task than erecting a skyscraper.

Realizing this, one rises to the challenge when they hear, "You can't kill an idea."

But still we will try!

Suppose the tribesmen had their own ideas. Spelled out on stone, they read something like: "Me Mountain God Demand Child Sacrifices Every Third Full Moon, Or Else There Be No Rain."

Then, most importantly, we want all those semi-unconscious minds—the ones sitting off to the side of the fire, too ignorant or cowardly to stand up and protest—to realize the insanity of the proposition: that no mountain god exists, and therefore can't trade natural occurrences for human blood. To make life there any better, or saner, the *idea itself* needs rebuking. If only the humans doing the killing were themselves killed, but the idea allowed to go unchallenged, and the rest of the tribe left alive, then the latter could possibly continue accepting the premise of the former, with unnecessary suffering thus rendered indefinite.

That sudden burst of hatred can be twofold: against the idea, and those who enact the idea. Nevertheless, hatred is needed in order to summon the courage that will bring permanent change. I'll venture a guess that some would likely give the okay to kill the tribe and to blow up their stone texts, thus putting an end to the barbaric ritual—unless those ideas were written down and put inside of some vessel or carrier, to be found later and taken up again by another primitive tribe.

Frustratingly, I can't find a part in the book where Robertson claims to "love" his culture. It's implied, but not said directly. A disagreement with such a proposition would be a rarity in either the alt-right or alt-light movements.

If that's granted, then we should acknowledge that culture is not just a race of people; it is an idea, or cluster of ideas, is it not? And if one can "love" their culture—as they can—then they can hate it, too. Robertson continues:

> *The people around us, just like objects and places, make us into who we are. Nearly every person alive has one particular teacher who made a lasting impression on us when we were younger. A lifetime of lasting impressions, of sage advice at critical junctures, of kept promises and fulfilled expectations, are the foundations of our personal growth and character development. The people with virtue—intelligence, skill, empathy, compassion, courage, curiosity, strength, loyalty and wisdom—make our lives better.*

Then the author discusses religiosity, specifically regarding families. Robertson argues that the parents of a hypothetical homosexual, who try to instill within him the fear of eternal damnation, actually love their son, because they don't want him to suffer in the afterlife.

Not noticing the contradiction of his earlier statement (hatred as defined by disgust towards *conscious mind*), Robertson writes that the homosexual son "hates the religion" (i.e., the ideas contained in the book) and that it "makes sense" for him to do so.

It does.

But on the illustration, I disagree again, this time with the motive of the parents. Not only can we hate ideas, we can also love those ideas *more* than we love our own children.

For the sincere believer in the doctrine of eternal damnation, the correct response is not myth-telling or fear-mongering. If one really believed that there was even the slightest possibility of their children ending up in Hell, the moral response ought to be anti-natalistic.

Someone consumed with absolute concern would never have children if they thought those children had even a 0.01% chance of being sentenced to eternal damnation. You would not have them, or if you did conceive them, you would terminate the fetus before that fetus had developed a brain capable of understanding, and thus rejecting, "god's love."

"What one cannot say, however, is that his family *hated him*, or any other gay," the author notes.

And that could be right: the parents of the homosexual

don't necessarily *hate* their son; they just love their god more than him. Similarly, Muslims who approve of murdering their children because they have left the faith (killing apostates is a mandate in Islam), if not downright hateful of their children, obviously love their god more than them.

Now, someone might reply that the religiously inclined love their children so much that they want them to spend an eternity in Heaven (or Paradise—pick your own poison).

Two thoughts on this.

1.) You can't logically love someone that isn't even here yet.

2.) If they were to take Matthew's gospel seriously, they would know that, "The highway to hell is broad, and its gate is wide for the many who choose the easy way. But the gateway to God's Kingdom is small, and the road is narrow, and only a few will ever find it." Therefore, these loving parents must realize that their children have a greater chance of being cast into Hell. Who would ever go to a casino and stake a bet with their children's lives? Some scumbag probably has done this, and we know what to say about them.

"If I were to guess, I would say that religion was not at fault," Robertson responds.

As to the crux of my contention, we return to the tribesman: as I see it, the hypocrisy of theism is the backbone of the idea. The mountain god worshippers are in the wrong, while those accepting the judgments of the Abrahamic god are in the right. Says the other distant tribe: "If you can have your

Skygod, we can have our Skygod."

This is not to say that religions are at all incomparable; Christians living today almost certainly have fewer archaic mandates than the majority of Muslims. Here, I find that Hatred towards one idea can be measured differently against another: I can freely exercise my own brand of hatred—peaceful speech and criticism—and not do so with the other. For one of these, violence doesn't enter into the picture at all.

I'll let the reader decide which of the respective faiths I am referring to.

Surely Robertson doesn't believe that every single last elder, parent, or priest has always done the best job possible when overseeing the younglings who they have been entrusted with. (Robertson quotes Molyneux a couple times, which should give some indication.) Again, this is something the author simply passes over, leaving us with a couple sentences in which we can infer from. "For most of us, spending time with these people can feel like the very reason for living," he writes, adding that: "The good people in your life are a part of your identity"—and then, like countercultural clockwork, concludes that "identity is everything." I would've thought that freedom or sustainability would be our everything, and I'm not quite sure if Robertson would say that those things followed from identity.

At what point would it be okay to hate, if not your elders or parents or priests, at least the ideas that they themselves were no doubt raised with? I've already given one example (religion) where I think such hatred is justified, and Robertson is in agreement with the homosexual son's feelings.

Indeed, we should be thankful that brave men and women throughout history have had the courage to hate *some* aspects of their culture, for this is the only way that humanity has seen improvement. It was *good* that people decided that they were no longer going to tolerate rule-by-monarchs, human sacrifices, foot binding, or any number of archaic ideals.

Does it not seem foolish to hate only those who sat on the throne or who pushed the lambs into the inferno, instead of hating what the crown and the fire had symbolized?

One doesn't necessarily need to burn the books that teach how to bind feet or how best to rule over a country; they only need to shout it from the bottom of their lungs: *this is wrong!*

Chapter Three

THIS IS NOT to say that hatred, as a sensible feeling or reaction that one might be able to make other people sympathize with, is applicative to every case imaginable. The time spent trying to explain to someone why you hated the planet Jupiter would likely not be granted by most. Loudly expressing your disdain for American cheese, and then professing your love for Swiss cheese, all while standing in front of both selections, would likewise come across as silly.

What about "places"?

One might feel hatred for the county that they were born and raised in; say, Los Angeles. With traffic congestion that is consistently rated as the worst in the U.S., and with heat waves that break records every 2 or 3 years, I really could not blame that person.

Says they: "It's too damn crowded, too damn hot, and there's so little to do for fun." Plus, they find themselves able to communicate with an increasingly smaller amount of people (the person doesn't speak Spanish). Now, I could just as well say that the person is "annoyed" or "irritated" by that part of the world, but when that person has actual dreams about "The Big One" (the imminent mythological earthquake that's taken quite seriously by a number of seismologists) suddenly capsizing the whole of Los Angeles and sending it far off into a watery grave out in the Pacific Ocean, I think to myself: *this is Hatred.*

And that doesn't make much sense. "Just pack up and leave." But if the legal circumstances were such that he was unable to leave, then we might hate the people who signed all the paperwork preventing that from happening. And what if those people had thought that they had the best intentions in mind? Who to hate then?

Still, the sprawling counties of Los Angeles are only but a dot on the map. Assuming that no such cuffs were in place, we would insist to that person that they take a bus or jump in the car and go elsewhere. This remedy would alleviate their suffering from the traffic and the heat, as many other regions have less cars and cooler climes.

This gets to the matter of monopoly.

If we can hate a place, what can we do about it?

How do we get away from a location if it's ruled over by a strong-arm of indeterminate length? If you hate the food or the management of a particular restaurant, you simply walk out the door and that's that.

Politically, once upon a time, decentralized power was a western principle of governance, and, if one didn't like the way their state or community was governing, they could "vote with their feet" and try another. In the age of globalization, technocracy, and corporatism, that idea has become difficult to envision.

Too many institutions, programs, peoples, and monies seem to be interconnected (a full study of these endless linkages is beyond the scope of this essay, but I'll try to touch on a couple examples). What if you hated the policies of an entire country—one that, even if seeing small differences from town to town, was still governed by a federally centralized state?

Here it might be more useful to hate the politicians who implemented such policies and sold the propaganda which reinforced them. This is because a country is much more than a government run by bureaucrats wearing nice suits; again, it would be silly to dwell on the hatred you have for a certain food or a different language.

But those bureaucrats wearing the nice suits are especially violent. Do their actions stem from love, or hate?

Let's look at just one of these gussied-up goblins: George Bush Jr., 43rd President of the United States. This man is a war criminal. There's no doubt in my mind about this. He is responsible for the needless deaths of thousands of Americans and millions of Iraqis. His motives were devoid of sincerity. At first, this implies Hatred. He must have *hated* those people, right? Not so fast. It could be worse than that: maybe Bush's motivation stemmed from indifference coupled with *love*.

Consider: prior to Bush even getting elected, officials and thinkers, many who would become members of his administration, had produced a document outlining a takeover of certain Middle Eastern countries. This was the Project for the New American Century, with Iraq mentioned specifically. After the Attacks of September 11th, Bush called for war against the regime of Saddam Hussein. Who can forget: "You're either with us, or you're with the terrorists"? People the world over were browbeaten without being given all the facts.

And there was a half dozen troubling facts that surrounded that event, some known back then and more found out later. It turned out that fifteen of the nineteen hijackers were Saudi Arabian citizens.

Saudi Arabia is ruled by a brutal regime, one that has been given longstanding support by Uncle Sam (with all U.S. presidents having obliged this continual doctrine). It also has a horrible human rights record, which did not make Bush 43 stop to reevaluate either that cozy comity, or his own personal business ties with the House of Saud. (One thing that Michael Moore got right). As well, members of the Saudi family were allowed to fly out of the country at a time when all other planes were ordered to remain grounded. The clincher: the notoriously redacted "28 Pages" of the 9/11 Commission report showed that at least a few of the hijackers had been financed by Saudi government officials.

Bush classified those sections.

And the next lie got us all into a war with a country and a regime that had nothing to do with the Attacks. Bush did this while still maintaining sodality with the Saudi's. Why would they do this? As cliché and simplistic as it might sound today, the real reason was—*and is*—because of oil. It was long known that Iraq had contained some of the last large reserves of petroleum, which were not being tapped to their full potential. Furthermore, Saddam was reported to be considering selling the oil exclusively in Euros, thereby undermining the hegemony of the dollar. Bush & Co. wanted to prevent this, and thereafter allow their favored corporations to reap the benefits.

Per a 2007 article published by *Counterpunch*, entitled "Bush Family War Profiteering," vice president Cheney's corporation, Halliburton, had received 60% of all the contracts in post-Saddam Iraq.[ii]

These contracts were worth millions of dollars.

Bush Sr. was a longtime board member of the Carlyle Group, a consulting firm also doing major business in Iraq. Listening to the condemnations of war profiteering, Bush Sr. resigned in 2003; it was later reported that he kept stock in the company, and also gave speeches for a half-million dollars. Other members of the Bush family had, too, lined their pockets with blood-soaked cash.

The president's uncle, William "Bucky" Bush sat on the board of Engineered Support System, a major military contractor that was also awarded contracts. In 2005, SEC filings showed that Bucky Bush made $450,000 by selling ESS stock, a figure that grew to $2.7 million the next year.

When learning about this deceptive warmongering and bloodthirsty profiteering, it becomes clear that Bush's main motivation was *love*—love for his own wealth, power, and dynasty.

In all likelihood, he didn't think anything of the innocent lives that were about to be extinguished. They were insects that a foot sometimes squishes while walking to the bank.

We can't say that it was a hatred of brown-skinned Arabs,

or of Islamists, or even the loving prospect of those people experiencing "freedom and democracy" (Bush's favorite nauseating utterances)—as we've seen Bush's friendship with one of the most repressive fundamentalist regimes in the region.

Bush would not have risked the chance of a war crimes tribunal if he had either loved, or despised, some oppressed Iraqis who had never threatened anything of value to him. In any case, Bush would not have let off the hook those Arabs who were currently tormenting their own population with the help of his Office, and who provided support to those who had attacked the country he was elected to preside over. Brushing that responsibility aside, Bush then did a McScrooge-like dive straight down into his vault of gold coins. This isn't to make excuses for Bush.

He's still a monster, but his reasons for war are much different than those of the Romans.

Before we continue, and lest I forget about our author, let me point out what I see to be another of his inconsistencies.

Recall that Robertson rebuffed any claim of hatred towards anything other than *conscious minds*. But later in the book, he gives a metaphor that's quite puzzling.

He writes:

> *In principle, places and objects become a part of who we are no less than our digits and limbs.*

He then cites the fabled Neolithic hunter-gatherer, who used a spear for everything from defense to hunting.

> *For all intents and purposes, it follows that the spear is a functional extension of his body, of his will.*

Robertson then grants that metaphor to a truck driver's rig, a marine's rifle, and a samurai's sword. These extensions, Robertson believes, are as attached to their owner as an arm or a leg.

Suddenly it's peachy to hate *anything*, so long as the inoperative object can be made functional by some person or group. As I take it, whoever exercises the greatest amount of influence over what would otherwise be azoic is acceptable for our disdain.

With that noted, let's continue.

One of the most potent forms of Hatred seen in the world today is that against *systems*—a monopoly of power and influence spread across a large area.

For instance, we hear enough about capitalism and fascism. (And not enough about communism, in my opinion.) As for Bush and the neoconservatives, we can dissect the system that brought about so many lies and profits and graves. President Bush—put there as he was by the American electorate—used his position as "commander of chief" of the U.S. armed forces to talk directly to both the nation and to the

United Nations.

His motivation was helped along by friendships long ago forged with those in his inner circle; namely, those in the defense industry, the oil companies, and the oil-rich Middle Eastern nations. In the latter part of his term, Bush began a vast surveillance program that has since spied on people all over the world. This was PRISM (the details of which brought to us by Edward Snowden).

Roughly speaking, when these many diffuse parts are assembled together, they form a "system of power." This is what makes voluntarism difficult to envision nowadays. Dissidents could no more escape being spied on than those Iraqi civilians could escape Bush's bombs. If they *really* want you, they'll either kill you, or keep an eye on you.

Yet, this is only one such system. For we in the English-speaking part of the world, living in what has become a blistering corporate parasite, should also be keeping our eyes on that other growing power, China.

That state also has favored corporations, a war machine, and a vast surveillance apparatus.

Chapter Four

ROBERTSON MAKES ONE point that is clear, correct, and useful.

> *[W]hile deeper understanding and empathy can sometimes remove false differences and opposition, it can just as often deepen the divide, and turn mere anger or incredulity into actual hatred.*

It's one of the most popular platitudes out there: that hatred stems from ignorance. It's widely believed that someone only hates something because they don't know enough about that which they hate.

On top of being erroneous, this claim is fantastically

arrogant.

In fact, hatred often develops specifically because one *has* learned something. Frequently, further intelligence will cultivate a more profound intolerance. Every new article is another step away, every book becomes a city block, and every personal experience a long train ride.

Thus, the distance between those whose brains have been wired differently grows wider. If Robertson's book has a single passage that makes it worth a purchase, that would be it.

"Tolerate people for who they are," says the transgender activist. Sounds doable—before one realizes how many transgender activists want to give puberty blockers to children suffering from gender dysphoria; who like to *de-platform* their critics while mandating proper pronoun usage; that think genital preferences are bigoted; and are okay with biological men playing and dominating female sports; and who launch "punch a TERF" campaigns.

This is hardly a mischaracterization of their goals, and it riles me into a state of opposition to what I see as child abuse, homophobia, biological obscurantism, and an assault on Free Speech.

Even then, you will sometimes hear someone assert their conflicting morals; the one who says that they *really do* believe in the freedom to say whatever you want, but will make it a point only when it's brought to their attention.

Before then, the original emphasis remains.

There is another *understanding* Robertson gives allusions

to, but doesn't use the precise wording.

Say it with me: Anti-White Hatred; i.e, *anti-racism*.

Observe the many statements, spectacles, and headlines. On CNN, commentator Symone Sanders is asked about a white man who was dragged out of his car and beaten to a pulp.

She shrugs snidely:

Oh my goodness, poor white people.

In a Q&A segment, stealth Sharia advocate and regressive icon Linda Sarsour was asked about her comments justifying the forced mutilation of Ayaan Hirsi Ali. Sarsour looks at the student, and wishes to *give some context* before answering.

And the context?

That the questioner happens to be a young white man. The lemmings applaud, content that female genital mutilation can be dismissed by merely calling attention to the skin color of the person making the charge.

The always verbose race hustler Michael Eric Dyson used nearly the exact same line on Jordan Peterson:

You're a mean, mad white man!

Laura [redacted]
White women should be hunted and killed then we won't get white babies who think the own the world!
WE NEVER GONA HAVE SOCIAL CHANGE TILL WE KILL ALL DA WHITE PEOPLE. #BlackLivesMatter
The Washington Times
Charles Hollins arrested in La Plata, Md. 'Kill all the white people' tweet:
don't you think it's a great opportunity to kill racist white people all at once at a
march? they all in one place
White Babies As Young As 6 Months Old Are Racist
Rod Dreher
When Is It OK To Kill Whites?
this kid literally brought a jug of water to class and is just drinking out of it. I hate college and i hate white people
#Mizzou black students need to stop protesting and start killing. The white supremacy made it clear they aint hearing it
All WHITES Needs Die . . This is a BLACKS WORLD
I honestly want every single trump supporter dead. This isn't a tweet for attention. If you support trump I want you 6 feet in the ground
SMASH THE WHITE MAN MARCH
IT'S OKAY TO BE WHITE
Newsweek
IS YOUR BABY RACIST?
How America has silently accepted the rage of white men
Science is embarrassingly white. That's a huge problem.
College Professor: Believing in Hard Work is White Ideology
"KILL ALL WHITE PEOPLE! Throw white babies into the fucking ocean or off a goddamn mountain! If you see a white person in the street stab them to death and watch the light fade from their racist eyes! Then go to their house and LIGHT THAT SHIT ON FIRE WITH THEIR FAMILY INSIDE! Enjoy their white tears and they slowly burn to death!"
Vox
White American men are a bigger domestic terrorist threat than Muslim foreigners
Im Racist I Dont Like White People
can't wait for november 4th when me and antifa buddies hit the streets to kill patriots all white people we find so the white race dies
White men must be stopped: The very future of mankind depends on it

In July of '18, the *New York Times* ran an article asking how best to *diversify* the state of New Hampshire, since the state is 94% white, and we can't have that. Later, the newspaper hired on a correspondent who tweeted incessantly about white people and their misdeeds.

A sample: "Its sick how much joy I get out of being cruel to old white men." In grodier venues, "comedian" Kristina Wong held a mock funeral for the "white man's penis," with several people pallbearing a large, stuffed, rather pale phallus off the stage. Elsewhere, black Harvard students argued that a full-blown genocide of white people might be a good idea, while professors have tweeted about their own white genocide fantasies. Of course, the last two are almost redundant, considering the kind of anti-white ideology being taught at many a university.

Notice that most of the examples given here are not from individuals posting on Twitter; these are said by well-known personalities, hosted by major institutions. And we know this is hatred because of the low standards that they themselves have set. As it is, the most subversive statement someone can make these days is "it's okay to be white." [iii]

Several universities decided to call the police when they found these fliers posted on their campuses, reporting it as "hate."

Some commentators argued the same.

How low can the bar go? Would it be seen as only a joke if anyone else had held a mock funeral for the black penis?

Would debates about black genocide be overlooked, let alone given a platform at such a prestigious university? If innocuous affirmations of one's own race or pigmentation can be deemed as hateful, then consistency should dictate what kind of finding if the roles were reversed and placed under these other scenarios?

This racial hatred is best evinced by the term "Intersectionality"—as in, the intersection of oppression: all the oppressed groups that have found the common denominator, the White Man. This activism lights up their hatred like a Broadway billboard, as any other crime committed by any other person is given a pass.

Now it's much easier to turn a blind eye to things like, say, transgender women raping biological women in penitentiaries that were originally designed for the latter. Or they'll say not a word about Islamic rape gangs that have targeted hundreds if not thousands of young girls in Europe. So much for homophobia in the black community, or anti-black racism in the Hispanic community. Who cares about that bigotry: those perpetrators are not cis-white-males, so they're not our enemy, and thus the crimes not our concern.

Or how many times do you see a white person on social media say something like, "White men disgust me," or "I wish white people would go away," and then you look at their profile and they have a young white male in their arms?

We can only guess that, once that child grows up into adulthood, they too will be hated. What's the point of even telling a white kid to do well in school when you also plan on insisting that their whole life is one big, unearned privilege? Going back to the religious reference, and the discussion about Hell, one might assume that an Intersectionalist who was so convinced that white people were privileged and held all the power would simply refrain from birthing this evil creature.

As can be seen, the Intersectional hatred of white men eclipses their professed love of women and children. After all, persons with penises can be women, just as much as all Muslims are part of an oppressed race of brown-skinned people. And all white males are privileged—unless they decide to become women, or maybe even a Muslim. See how that works?

Any observer of the culture wars can attest to how rampant this sentiment is. There's an entire segment of society that springs out of their beds every morning looking to see what evil the white man has wrought today. How do I feel about it? I'm upset. It makes me angry. But not because of the overt racism. For I would never want to hinder someone's expression of Hatred. It is their right to harbor whatever feelings they wish to. No: what upsets me is their *dishonesty*.

Generally, these are the same people who scold others when perceiving *them* to be harbingers of hatred, perhaps seen most clearly whenever they condemn so-called "hate speech." They raise signs that laughingly read: "Love Trumps Hate." They shout that there's "only one race—the human race." Then they finalize by saying: "We don't debate Nazis...and everyone, regardless of their skin color, who believes in immigration controls, or any white person who recognizes the importance of homogeneity...is a Nazi." And this while ignoring the prejudices and cultural proclivities of other groups; i.e., "Nothing bothers me except the white man who doesn't acknowledge his privilege." (Well, at least Gandhi is finally getting some heat.)

They have the audacity to preach about *inclusion* and *tolerance*, with no shame in scratching their heads and asking why separatist/identitarian movements are once again becoming vogue amongst the American citizenry. The phenomenon was captured wonderfully by Christian satire site Babylon Bee: "Movement That Demands Forceful Silencing of

All Opposing Viewpoints Unsure Why Nation So Divided."
Quote:

> *"It just doesn't make any sense," one opinion
> writer at Slate wrote, in an article entitled
> "Why Can't We All Just Get Along and Also
> Agree with Me or I Will Kill You?" Why can't
> our nation get along? Also, if you breathe an
> opinion even slightly different from our own,
> we will destroy you. But yeah, let's all be
> united and stuff.*

Case in point: for the last couple of years, we've seen peaceful
protesters get bashed in the head with bike-locks, punched in
the face, and tear gassed.

Despite what is said, many of those victims were
commonplace conservatives who believe in things once on the
table for discussion (like immigration controls and abortion
restrictions). Still, the response from these Intersectionalists—
and their patrons on CNN and MSNBC—has been either
encouragement or silence.

But, when the president comes out and criticizes violence
on "both sides," [iv] they all suddenly find themselves without
gravity. Right before the tears of anger and hatred begin to
gush, they wonder why someone would risk scrambling their
circuitry by making such an honest and ecumenical statement.

"*Both sides?!*" they squeal, "But we've only been saying

'punch a Nazi' for these many months, while labeling virtually everybody a Nazi."

How could anybody aside from an impartial observer wonder why they would be so shocked by this? Why can it not just be admitted that, yes, they have been calling for violence; and, yes, there were violent Antifa members in Charlottesville during the "Unite the Right" protest? *Acknowledge* the hatred. Be brave with it.

As we saw earlier, such hypocrisy serves as the backbone for a new form of theism, which is exactly what John McWhorter has argued that "anti-racism" has become. "If they can be racist, I can be racist"—says every Intersectionalist and every white supremacist now set in hate-driven perpetuity. So much for MLK's colorblindness.

This is not to say that America started out with everybody hating whitey.

Quite the opposite, and to put it mildly, of course. But then one will hear the corollary: "We're not against white people, we're against *whiteness.*"

The system! Or culture. Or both.

What a great failsafe, a sort of Get-Out-of-Hate-Free-Card. As if it's possible to separate the two.

After all, what is *whiteness*? Is it the Bill of Rights? The Washington Monument? The English language? Well, it can't be the last, as Europeans have multiple languages, and they still get called *racist* often enough.

Even so, the first is something that I'd prefer to keep

around. The answer is probably found in the second—
monuments, the statues of tyrannical white people. Add that
to the calls of "privilege" (white people benefiting from mere
existence in this society) and it's clear: their hatred *must* be
attached to sentient persons in the here and now.

And, as Robertson writes:

> *This hesitancy to admit feeling hatred induces a*
> *pallid dishonesty, filled with lame defenses that*
> *do not convince anyone.*

Nobody that I've ever seen, anyway.

Chapter Five

IN THESE CHANGING times, in the age of mass information and mass movement, with morals and standards now shifting and dissolving away, we can guess how much bumpier the terrain is going to get.

Persuasion is already too often like two people using a tin-cup telephone, with one receiver on earth and the other on the moon, and then trying to debate the merits of quantum physics. We find that the chances of reconciliation between people with differing convictions is all but zero.

The Great Day of Acceptance, therefore, will not soon peak over the horizon. The Kumbaya Theory, tested and tried, is still left unproven. Funerals, flowers, and the flow of time are things that will happen long before the great masses come to embrace universal understanding.

Religion is harmful and false! says the anti-theist.

No, says the religiously-inclined, it is based on love and truth. Islam is predicated on war, conversion, and subjugation, says the secular humanist. But look at what Christians have done! a Regressive Lefty quips, while not acknowledging important things like the Enlightenment, the Virginia Statute, and the secular law of the West.

Well, think of all those western white men that purport to be followers of Christ but who blow up kids in other parts of the world, insists the more serious liberal. Agreed, but it's also true that Islam has its own bloody history, and, unlike Western society today, Muslim societies do not have the corrective mechanism of free speech and protest.

War! Says I: America's foreign aggression is always based on lies and fought for resources, not national security.

No, Iraq was responsible for 9/11 and needed to get bombed, says the jingoist, adding that all those dozens of countries that America has bombed since the mid-20th century were deserving of that destruction. But, adds the critical thinker, what about Democracy?

After all, while most presidential administrations have been run by white men, who gives sanction to their power? But white people are not the only ones who go out to the polls and vote. People of color are quite vociferous in their political choices, yes? Even if it's true that politicians appeal to the masses in order to win elections, and then go and renege on virtually everything they had promised, it's much harder for them to get into that office and accomplish their lies without popular support. Then who else is to be held responsible for, say, Obama having killed more civilians in the Middle East than Bush had (according to The Bureau of Investigative Journalism)[v]

Did black America and Latino America not help to elect him?

It's child abuse to prevent your prepubescent kid from transitioning! shouts the transgender activist. You know, says the majority, "I feel like a boy" or "I feel like a girl" are *not* valid reasons to experiment on a healthy and developing endocrine system. What do you care what other people do!? the first person screams loudly again. With hands raised and eyes squinted, the second person simply points out the ironies: that *refusing* to make permanent alterations on a child's body is now seen by scores of people as a form of abuse, and that "not caring what other people do" can be said for just about anything else.

Islamophobe! Anti-Semite!—thereby deploying the cleverest trick in the book: conflating one's actions with one's race. Any criticism of these two religions gets an accusation of racism, prompting the logical question: "What race is Christianity?"

The anti-theists and secularists can't win any argument as long as the hurdle is set that high. They'll always have to defend against the charge that they're critical of *immutable characteristics* rather than *conscious action.* This is something that is lost on the Intersectionalists, as they constantly decry "white people" while defending Islam—despite the obvious differentiation that's just been made.

The System!

Yes, there's been a white supremacist system, and it has caused some harm and suffering. But it's also one of many that have existed throughout human history. And now, we can see the emergence of an Asiatic superpower. Environmentalists will find horror at the fact that the Chinese industrial base is the largest emitter of CO_2 in the world.

More than that, the Chinese have muscled their way into Africa. Domestically, their government detains and monitors hundreds of thousands of Uyghurs, a Muslim minority. So then, when we hear that "white people are the worst/most destructive/least caring"—we know that the person uttering those words is so consumed with Hatred that they are blinded to reality.

At last I will defend the eponymous title of my essay.

For I do not believe that love and tolerance can sort these contentions out. Only Hatred can signal the "moral pulse"—as Robertson puts it—to effectuate what I believe to be the proper solution.

To answer the question posed at the beginning, I think Robertson is expecting a second civil war in America.

Witnessing all the random scuffles on the streets between AntiFa, "alt-rightists," and "alt-lighters," it's not hard to see why he would think this. However, in another part of his book, Robertson writes: "Like disgust, hatred leads to destruction"—*or*—"distance."

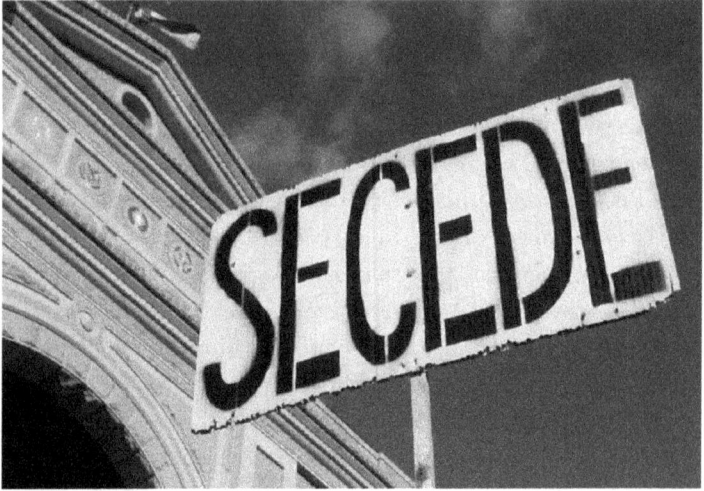

Here I am hopeful, as I do not like the prospect of violence. Instead, we need even more division, more discord, and more fragmentation. The moronic Intersectional idiom is: "He/They are trying to divide us!" As if human beings don't already divide themselves in all sorts of ways, and without the help of anybody else.

Unfortunately, the new state religion of "multiculturalism" makes it difficult to actualize on broader levels.

Thankfully, the other big conversation being had today is

in regards to borders, with the national kind getting a lot of attention. What I have noticed is that most people who talk about national borders will set their focus solely on the American scene, while ignoring the importance of borders *per se.*

For example, plenty of anarchists will make post after endless post labeling everyone a sadistic statist who believes that America's southern border be made secure.

Fine.

Detainment is violence and violence is bad. So then, if this is a level of aggression on par with, say, genocide (such people often get called fascists), then the conviction should be carried outward to newer regions. America is not the only country with national borders, nor are Americans the only people who care about the concept. (Imagine all those fascists in the world!)

There are opportunities for this. Note how many American anarchists attend the event "Anarchapulco," the big annual gathering of liberty-minded folks that's held down in Mexico.

We should hope to hear at least one speaker get on the stage and pronounce that the Mexicans who recently protested the caravan of South American immigrants are, as much as any redneck American, violent statists who cannot morally control all of the land.[vi] Perhaps this has been said, but I'm unaware and will make the correction if it happens.

Or, as another option, these anarchists could pool some

money together and do some St. Francis-like proselytizing around the globe. This trend could have begun last year, when Jeffrey Tucker went to visit Israel.

Tucker, with characteristic glee, had praised the beautiful freedom of being able to drink alcohol out on the public street. Sounds great to me! But having previously recounted a time in which Murray Rothbard had refused to work with a group of nationalists, this because of their rejection of "universals," "truth," and "human rights," thinking that "everything is tribal and biological"—and with Tucker in apparent agreement of this appraisal—I was expecting him to have a stronger condemnation of Israel's borders.[vii]

Tucker's response to me:

> *I feel odd about going to Israel and lecturing people about a political system I do not understand. I wouldn't do that in New Zealand or Ireland either. So I think I'll stick with what I know, which are general principles, among which freedom of movement.*

So much for the Palestinians.

Presumably, Tucker will continue to single out Americans. Ditto for the rest of the vocal no-border anarchists.

Which is a bit cowardly, considering that "Doctors Without Borders" and "Reporters Without Borders" are two groups that routinely travel to other regions whenever there's a serious conflict.

And, since detainment of migrants obviously constitutes a true-and-true conflict, and since many of these anarchists make the statement that the "government doesn't protect your rights anyway," these anarchists should get moving.

But they won't.

They'll stay right here and say these things where there's no risk, and probably won't say it even when they do travel abroad. This is what I'll call an *under-performative contradiction.*

Then there's the regressive leftists, who have been protesting the separation of Mexican families. These protestations often stem from the premise that, since white Europeans came here and took the land from the natives, the only proper atonement is to dissolve the borders altogether and to let whomever in ("nobody is illegal on stolen land").

But notice the ensuing contradiction: these same people will then argue for an elimination of the electoral college, thus increasing the possibility that the people living in Aztlán (a term used to designate the stolen southwestern territory) will elect the president of *these* United States (and while it's not a guarantee that California will elect a liberal POTUS, there is an increased likelihood).

Therefore, the stolen regions are *illegitimate* when seen as part of the greater nation, but then *legitimate* when the correct politics are involved. Moreover, many that I've

41

generalized here will condemn government agents who separate families at the border, but then praise the work of IRS agents whenever they arrest someone for tax evasion—those splintered families be damned! (and imagine if said-tax resister does so explicitly because they had refused to subsidize another culture!)

They'll then ask for federal programs that benefit the people living in mythical Aztlán, and sometimes at the expense of those who live elsewhere in the U.S. (it's called redistributionism). Again, central government bad when national sovereignty; central government good when socialism for everybody who manages to get over here.

But maybe this is their pragmatism, which, despite being something of a digression, brings me to my point on the border question.

We all believe in borders.

Those who say "I can't see borders from outer space" forget to mention that neither can you see your backyard fence either. But it's there. And those who say they don't believe in any walls at all—*are lying.* As with people who lock their doors at night, those who oppose mass migration don't necessarily *hate* those who they're restricting into an area; they just love those who they already share a language, culture, and history with. Yet another perspective that will never be universally shared.

Borders can be seen as the symbolic representation of Stay Away. My belief is that there need not be civil war if we all embraced borders that were, if not more physical, then more philosophic.

You'll notice I haven't tried to define hatred.

I've only said where I think it can apply—to almost anything. For the person who hates Los Angeles, they probably don't hate every person living there. It's a combination of factors that led to the feelings they have—the urge to want to *get away.* Integration and harmony might come to us some day. But in the meantime, we need a means to express the views we hold dear, and to help us eliminate the external barriers that prevent us from separating more broadly in the real world.

Technology and mass communication has allowed for this plan. Uncountable platforms have been raised from inside the sanctity of one's own living room, with little reason to travel to the speaker's corner, Congress or the radio station.

Looking at it another way, social media is the panopticon evolved into its final form. The cells are voluntary: one doesn't have to put all their information up online.

Thus, the NSA has much less work to do than the 20th century guardsmen. And for right now, the average citizen can peer into other people's open windows and listen to what they're saying. People, it seems, are still quite Hateful.

Am I the only one who has noticed how many of those with strong opinions make frequent use of block and delete buttons? Not that social media is at all comparable to nations and cities and houses, but the irony of it still stands out. When there's no risk at all, the "Go-The-Fuck-Away-Forever" option is only one click away. "Tolerance" and "diversity of opinion" is discarded at an instant. This is great!

Our hate-filled assessments can transcend walls while still maintaining them. We don't need a mere defense of hatred— we must also be in *favor* of hatred.

How often do you see someone who says that they're opposed to something, but won't risk offending someone who does or advocates for the thing they're opposing? Celebrities, for instance, get away with an assortment of crimes that would otherwise result in alienation by lesser-valued people.

The virtue signaler, safely raging against the moral crime on their social media outlets, but still seeking a high status in the realer world, will forget all about those crimes the moment it's time to take a picture with said-celebrity.

Or, the "Love No Matter What" crowd will refuse to interrogate any new friends regarding their convictions— because everyone is a good person as long as you know nothing about them. This indicates that, to them, the crimes they were raging against are not all that intolerable.

GOOD... GOOD...

LET THE HATE FLOW THROUGH YOU

In the end, I hope that the Hateful will not inherit the earth. Nevertheless, Robertson writes a line that I myself have uttered many times, long before even hearing about his book: "None of that matters; my hatred is valid. Your hatred is not."

It's always the other person's Hatred that's wrong and unjust. My own is just fine.

So, instead of embarking on a futile quest for universal love, let us all embrace our Hatred. Let our Hatred runneth over. Post your favorite Islamophobic memes, your anti-Semitic memes, your transphobic memes, your anti-white memes. Celebrate the death of a warmongering ex-president. Wish for the privileged men to die in traffic, and maybe some nutty feminist too. Infuriate a veteran who killed for oil companies.

Call out the hypocrisy of bordertarians.

Likewise the insincerity of those on the other side. Tell a theocrat what for! Don't forget the police and the pedophiles. Doxx someone; meet the protesters outside your house with a Gatling gun. This will sting a bit. There could be a panic attack, or two.

Always keep in mind what is at stake here: peaceful coexistence.

Through this process, we will learn to separate ourselves on even broader levels. Libertarian theory says that people should not be forced to associate, nor to pay, for anything that they hate; as well, they should be allowed to secure their earnings and their time for those that they do love.

If we could just be consistent with these principles, we will see a better world. With this expression allowed to run freely, we will all reap the benefits of constructive hatred—the harsh criticisms of ideas, persons, and oppressive systems.

They will penetrate even the most impenetrable walls, and force change from within. If structures were granted complete sovereignty, people who agree will migrate to those areas if they are allowed, or mimic them when building their own.

Others excluded will go elsewhere.

As for moral standards, culture and behavior will change to what makes the most sense. Perhaps there will be a small community that codifies Sharia law while still hosting Pride Parades. Like the existence of god or the Easter bunny, it's possible.

Like fresh cream and good ideas, quality Hatred will rise to the top.

End Notes

[i] https://www.amazon.com/Defense-Hatred-C-B-Robertson/dp/1520526016

[ii] https://www.counterpunch.org/2007/04/12/bush-family-war-profiteering/

[iii] https://www.cbc.ca/news/canada/manitoba/hate-messages-university-manitoba-campus-1.4889084

[iv] https://www.youtube.com/watch?v=j9AYhdKTe1w

[v] https://www.thebureauinvestigates.com/stories/2017-01-17/obamas-covert-drone-war-in-numbers-ten-times-more-strikes-than-bush

[vi] https://www.theguardian.com/world/2018/nov/19/mexico-protests-grow-in-tijuana-against-migrant-caravan

[vii] https://archive.org/details/DerrickBrozeAndJeffreyTuckerTheConsciousResistance

www.ingramcontent.com/pod-product-compliance
Lightning Source LLC
Chambersburg PA
CBHW031542040426
42445CB00010B/658